Native American Life

The Northeast Indians

Daily Life in the 1500s

by Janeen R. Adil

Consultant:
Troy Rollen Johnson, PhD
American Indian Studies
California State University
Long Beach, California

Capstone *press*

Mankato, Minnesota

Bridgestone Books are published by Capstone Press,
151 Good Counsel Drive, P.O. Box 669, Mankato, Minnesota 56002.
www.capstonepress.com

Library of Congress Cataloging-in-Publication Data
Adil, Janeen R.
    The Northeast Indians: daily life in the 1500s / by Janeen R. Adil.
    p. cm.—(Bridgestone books. Native American life)
    Summary: "A brief introduction to Native American tribes of the Northeast, including their social
structure, homes, food, clothing, and traditions"—Provided by publisher.
    Includes bibliographical references and index.
    ISBN 0-7368-4314-0 (hardcover)
    1. Indians of North America—Northeastern States—History—16th century—Juvenile literature.
2. Indians of North America—Northeastern States—Social life and customs—16th century—Juvenile
literature. 3. Northeastern States—Antiquities—Juvenile literature. I. Title. II. Series.
E78.E2A35 2006
974.004'97—dc22   2005001654

Editorial Credits

Christine Peterson, editor; Jennifer Bergstrom, set designer; Ted Williams, book designer;
    Jo Miller, photo researcher/photo editor; maps.com, map illustrator

Photo Credits

Canadian Museum of Civilization/by Roberta Wilson/photo by Harry Foster /D2004-18606, 6
The Granger Collection, New York, 8, 10
Mary Evans Picture Library, 18, 20
Superstock, cover, 12, 14; Newberry Library, 16

1 2 3 4 5 6 10 09 08 07 06 05

Table of Contents

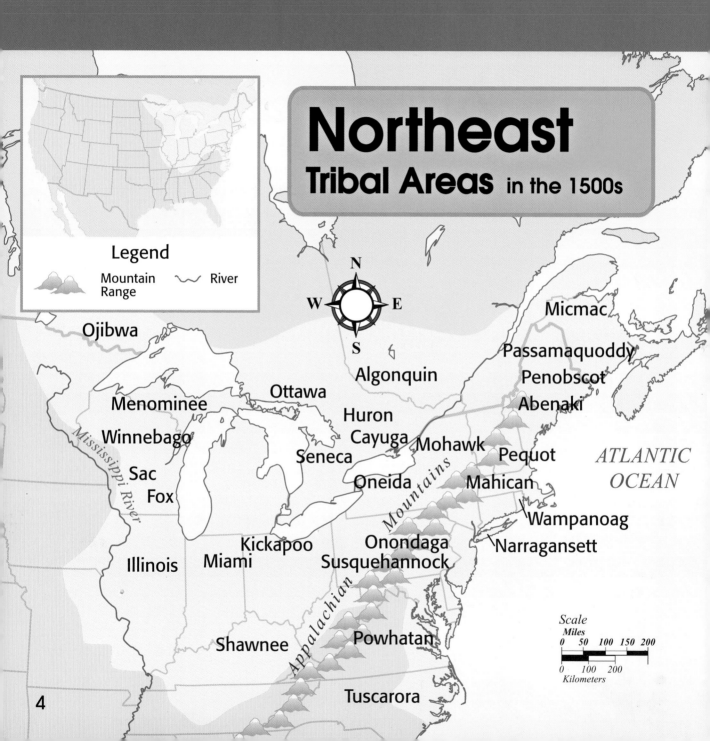

Northeast
Tribal Areas in the 1500s

Legend

Mountain Range

River

Ojibwa

Micmac

Passamaquoddy

Penobscot

Algonquin

Abenaki

Ottawa

Menominee

Huron

Winnebago

Cayuga

Mohawk

Pequot

ATLANTIC OCEAN

Seneca

Sac

Oneida

Mahican

Fox

Mississippi River

Kickapoo

Onondaga

Wampanoag

Illinois

Miami

Susquehannock

Narragansett

Mountains

Appalachian

Shawnee

Powhatan

Scale
Miles
0   50   100 150 200

0   100   200
Kilometers

Tuscarora

The Northeast and Its People

In the 1400s and 1500s, many Native American tribes lived in the thick forests of the Northeast. This area stretches from what is now Maine to North Carolina. It is bordered by the Mississippi River to the west and the Atlantic Ocean in the east. Native Americans have lived there for at least 10,000 years.

When European explorers arrived in the 1500s, many tribes were **thriving**. The land provided materials for homes, tools, and clothing. Tribes hunted and fished for food. The woodlands shaped their daily life.

◄ Historic Northeast tribal areas are shown over the present-day borders of the United States and Canada.

Social Structure

Northeast Indians lived in large family groups called **clans**. Clans lived in the same village. Many clans made up a tribe. Each tribe had its own language. Chiefs led most tribes with help from a council.

At least 500 years ago, some tribes joined together to form a nation. The Mohawk, Oneida, Onondaga, Cayuga, and Seneca formed the Iroquois **Confederacy**. In 1722, the Tuscarora joined the confederacy. The confederacy made decisions about trade, agreements with other tribes, and war.

◀ Clans often lived together in one home. Each family had its own small area to live and sleep.

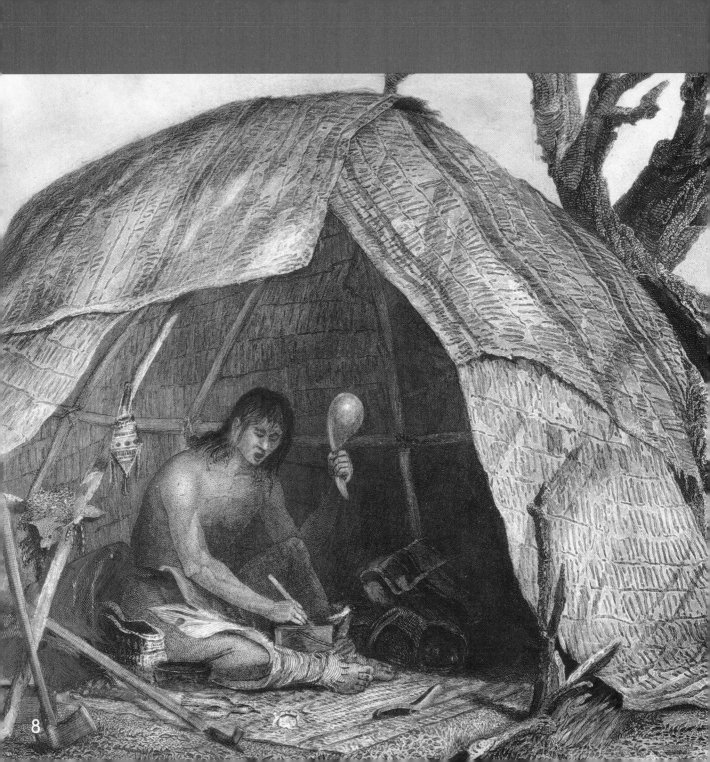

Homes

Native American tribes used young trees to build their homes. The Abenaki and other tribes lived in houses called **wigwams**. They framed these homes with young trees and covered them with birch bark. When tribes moved, they rolled up the birch bark covers. They left the frames behind.

Tribes like the Iroquois and Huron lived in large **longhouses**. Bark from elm trees covered the walls and roof. Most tribes lived in longhouse villages all year.

◄ Native Americans peeled large sheets of bark from birch trees to cover the wood frames of wigwams.

Food

The land and waters of the Northeast were full of good things to eat. Men hunted ducks and turkeys. They caught salmon in rivers.

Women gathered food from the land. They collected berries, honey, and nuts. The Ojibwa gathered wild rice. Wild rice was ground to make bread. It was also popped like popcorn.

Many tribes grew crops for food. Corn, beans, and squash were the main crops. Tribes called these crops the "Three Sisters." Some crops and gathered foods were dried for winter meals.

◄ Ojibwa women beat stalks of wild rice plants with wooden paddles to harvest the rice.

12

Clothing

The Northeast tribes made clothing from skins of animals, like rabbits, deer, and bears. Their clothing matched the weather. When it was warm, women wore skirts. Men wore **breechcloths**. When it was cold, men added leggings, and women wore long dresses. Everyone wore warm robes of fur and animal skins.

People often walked through the forests with bare feet. When they wore shoes, they put on moccasins. These soft shoes were made of animal skins.

◀ Northeast Native Americans used animal fur and skins to make robes, leggings, skirts, and other clothing.

Trading and Economy

Tribes traded with each other for goods they could not get in their areas. Tribes usually traded furs, tools, shells, and corn.

The Narragansett gathered **whelk** and **quahog** shells along the coast. They used the shells to make purple and white beads called **wampum**. The Narragansett traded wampum for goods from other tribes.

The Ottawa were known for their trading. The name Ottawa means "traders." They traded furs and medicines for other goods.

◀ The Narragansett wove wampum beads into colorful belts. These belts were popular trade items.

Leisure Time

Northeast tribes often played outdoor games. Nature provided the materials. Many tribes played stickball. This game is also called lacrosse. In winter, the Penobscot played snow snake. To play, tribes made an icy track in the snow. Players slid a wooden stick along the track to see how far it would go.

Children played games to learn about their tribe's way of life. Boys learned to hunt using small bows and arrows made from wood. Girls practiced child care with dolls made from cornstalks or cattails.

◀ Native Americans often played stickball, or lacrosse, on the icy rivers of the Northeast.

Traditions

In the Northeast, tribes held ceremonies to celebrate the seasons. Most tribes held a Green Corn Ceremony in late summer. They held this ceremony when the first ears of corn were ready to harvest. The celebration lasted four days.

Tribes celebrated the harvest with games, songs, and dances. In the Feather Dance, men wore many feathers and thanked the earth for good crops. Women made special foods. A favorite food, succotash, was made with corn and beans.

◄ Tribes danced and gave thanks for a good harvest during the Green Corn Ceremony.

Passing On Traditions

Tribes passed on their history and beliefs by telling stories. During the long winter nights, people sat by the fire to tell stories. Elders told stories about the tribe's history and traditions.

Some stories were about heroes. Passamaquoddy children enjoyed hearing about the great Gluskabe. In one story, Gluskabe shoots an arrow at an ash tree. When the bark splits, the earth's first people come out. By telling this story, tribes shared their history and way of life with others.

◀ Fathers often told stories to teach their children about the tribe's past and traditions.

Glossary

breechcloth (BREECH-kloth)—a short, skirtlike garment that is tied around the waist and has open slits on the sides

clan (KLAN)—a large group of related families

confederacy (kuhn-FED-ur-uh-see)—a union of towns or tribes with a common goal

longhouse (LAWNG-houss)—a large house made from young trees and bark

quahog (KWAW-hawg)—a clam with a thick, heavy shell

thrive (THRIVE)—to do well and flourish

wampum (WAHM-puhm)—beads made from polished shells strung together or woven to make belts

whelk (WELK)—a large snail that lives in salt water and has a spiral shell

wigwam (WIG-wahm)—a round house covered with tree bark

Read More

Ansary, Mir Tamim. *Eastern Woodlands Indians.* Native Americans. Chicago: Heinemann, 2000.

Yue, Charlotte, and David Yue. *The Wigwam and the Longhouse.* Boston: Houghton Mifflin, 2000.

Internet Sites

FactHound offers a safe, fun way to find Internet sites related to this book. All of the sites on FactHound have been researched by our staff.

Here's how:
1. Visit *www.facthound.com*
2. Type in this special code **0736843140** for age-appropriate sites. Or enter a search word related to this book for a more general search.
3. Click on the **Fetch It** button.

FactHound will fetch the best sites for you!

Index